5

D0442953

ATOS Book Level: ___2.3___
AR Points: ___0.5___
Quiz #: _105 710_ ☑RP☐ LS☐ VP
Lexile: _____

Read-About® Math

Math Tools

By Melanie Chrismer

Consultants
Chalice Bennett
Elementary Specialist
Martin Luther King Jr. Laboratory School
Evanston, Illinois

Ari Ginsburg
Math Curriculum Specialist

Children's Press®
A Division of Scholastic Inc.
New York   Toronto   London   Auckland   Sydney
Mexico City   New Delhi   Hong Kong
Danbury, Connecticut

Designer: Herman Adler Design
Photo Researcher: Caroline Anderson
The photo on the cover shows peppers on a scale.

Library of Congress Cataloging-in-Publication Data

Chrismer, Melanie.
  Math tools / by Melanie Chrismer.
    p. cm. — (Rookie read-about math)
  ISBN 0-516-24961-4 (lib. bdg.)   0-516-25550-9 (pbk.)
  1. Measuring instruments—Juvenile literature. I. Title. II. Series.
  QC100.5.C47 2006
  681'.2—dc22
                                    2005019972

CHILDREN'S PRESS, and ROOKIE READ-ABOUT®,
and associated logos are trademarks and/or registered trademarks
of Scholastic Library Publishing. SCHOLASTIC and associated logos
are trademarks and/or registered trademarks of Scholastic Inc.

1 2 3 4 5 6 7 8 9 10 R 15 14 13 12 11 10 09 08 07 06

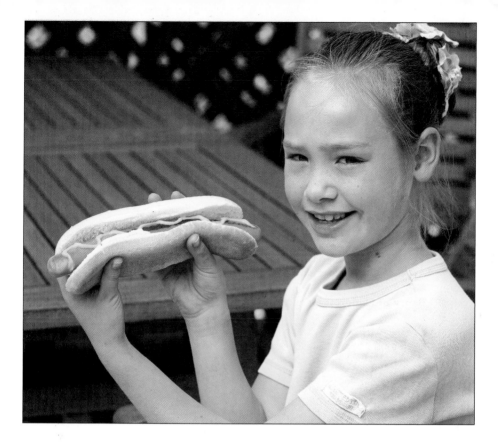

It's hard to measure things
with a foot-long hot dog.
Use a math tool instead.

There are many math tools.

Math tools help you measure and count.

Math tools make math easier.

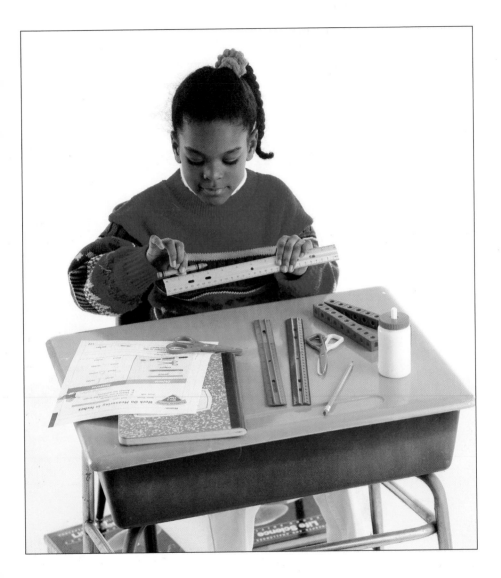

6

A ruler is a math tool.

A ruler measures how long something is.

A ruler measures length.

Some rulers measure in
inches. There are 12 inches
in 1 foot.

Rulers are great.

A ruler cannot measure the amount of milk inside a glass.

A measuring cup can.

A measuring cup is a math tool.

Measuring cups measure the space taken up by a liquid or anything that can be poured.

Measuring cups measure volume (VOL-yuhm).

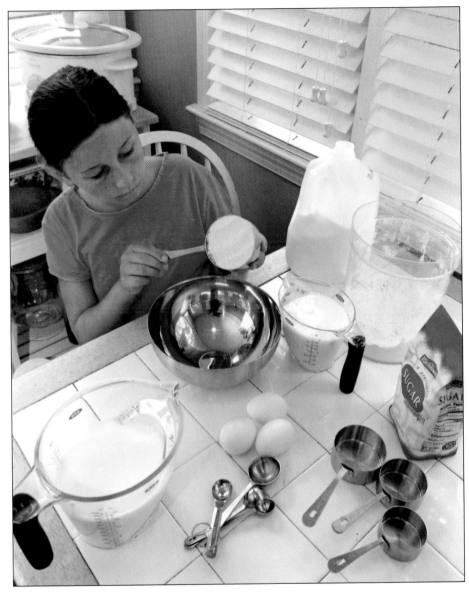

11

Some measuring cups measure in ounces. There are 8 ounces in 1 cup.

Measuring cups are great.

A measuring cup cannot
tell you if you have a fever.

A thermometer
(thur-MOM-uh-tur) can.

A thermometer is a math tool.

A thermometer tells you how hot or cold something is.

A thermometer measures temperature (TEM-pur-uh-chur).

This thermometer shows that the weather is warm.

Thermometers measure
temperature in degrees.
A higher degree number
means a hotter temperature.

Thermometers are great.

A thermometer cannot
tell you if you are on
time for school.

A clock can.

A clock is a math tool.

A clock tells you what time it is.

A clock counts time.

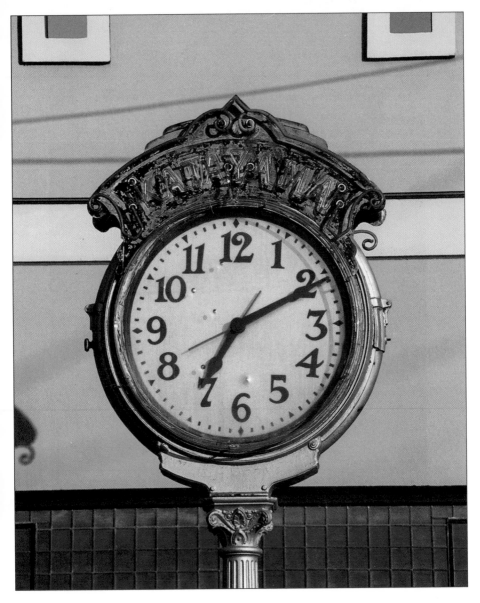

A clock counts in seconds, minutes, and hours. The hands on a clock point to the time.

Clocks are great.

A clock cannot tell you how many days there are until your birthday.

A calendar can.

A calendar is a math tool.

A calendar shows the order of days. It shows past days, today, and future days.

A calendar shows the days, weeks, and months of the year.

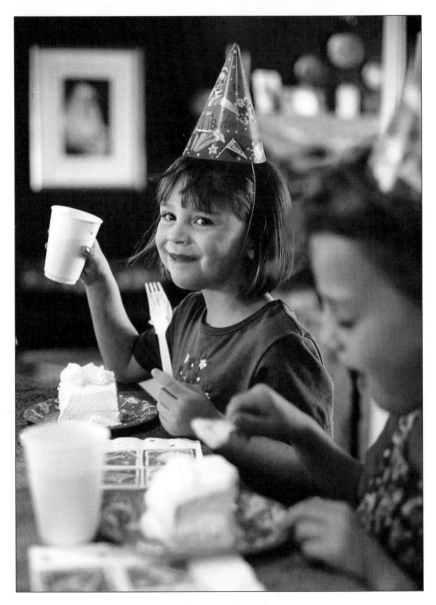

Calendars are great.

A calendar can tell you when your birthday is coming.

It cannot tell you that you weigh more than you did last year.

A scale can.

A scale is a math tool.

A scale tells you how heavy something is.

A scale measures weight.

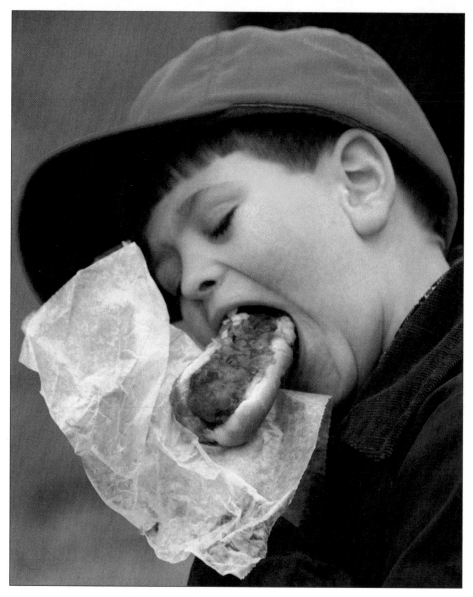

Foot-long hot dogs are great to eat.

Math tools are great for counting and measuring.

Words You Know

calendar

clock

hot dog

measure

measuring cup

ruler

scale

thermometer

31

Index

About the Author

Melanie Chrismer is a writer and flutist who lives near Atlanta, Georgia. She loves reading, writing, and eating foot-long hot dogs with lots of mustard.

Photo Credits